DESERTS

THIS EARTH OF OURS

Mel Higginson

The Rourke Corporation, Inc.
Vero Beach, Florida 32964

Edited by Sandra A. Robinson

PHOTO CREDITS
© Mel Higginson: cover, title page, pages 4, 8, 10, 13, 15, 21;
courtesy Egyptian Tourist Authority: pages 7, 17; courtesy
Phoenix Convention Bureau: page 18; © Jerry Hennen: page 12

Library of Congress Cataloging-in-Publication Data

Higginson, Mel, 1942-
    Deserts / by Mel Higginson.
    p. cm. — (This earth of ours)
    Includes index.
    ISBN 0-86593-380-4
1. Desert ecology—Juvenile literature. 2. Deserts—Juvenile
literature. [1. Desert ecology. 2. Ecology.] I. Title. II. Series:
Higginson, Mel, 1942-   This earth of ours.
QH541.5.D4H54
574.5'2652—dc20   94-9403
                                                          CIP
                                                          AC

Printed in the USA

TABLE OF CONTENTS

DESERTS

Deserts are the world's dry lands. The great Sahara Desert usually has less than three inches of rain per year!

Deserts may be hot or cold. Some are nearly lifeless, but others are quite green at times.

The driest deserts have the fewest plants, animals and people. Moister deserts, like the Sonoran in Arizona and northern Mexico, have a greater variety of life.

The Sonoran Desert has a wide variety of plants and animals

WHERE DESERTS ARE

Deserts cover one-fifth of the Earth's land surface, according to some scientists. The largest desert is the Sahara Desert in North Africa. The Sahara is about seven times larger than North America's 500,000 square miles of desert. North American deserts are in the western United States and in parts of Mexico.

Many scientists consider the dry lands of northernmost Canada and Antarctica to be cold deserts.

The largest of the world's deserts is the Sahara of North Africa

LIFE OF THE DESERT

The desert is **habitat,** or home, for many plants and animals that don't live anywhere else.

The best-known plants of North American deserts are cactus. In the United States, the biggest cactus is the saguaro. Cactus do well in dry climates because they can store water.

After a spring rain, a desert may bloom with colorful wildflowers. Warm spring days also bring animals from hiding.

Desert animals, such as tortoises, lizards, snakes and rodents, are usually **nocturnal,** or active at night. Desert nights are much cooler than desert days.

Spring rains bring the dry desert to life

HOW ANIMALS LIVE IN THE DESERT

By hunting at night, desert animals save energy and water. At night, their bodies don't overheat. Desert animals such as badgers, kangaroo rats and spadefoot toads spend hot summer days in shady burrows.

Desert animals all have special ways to use their habitat and survive. The cactus wren builds its nest among the spines of cholla cactus. The elf owl nests in holes punched into cactus by gila woodpeckers.

A cactus wren, untouched by the spines, perches by its nest in a cholla cactus

*Hot, dry Death Valley National Monument is part of the
Mojave Desert in California*

The night-loving sand cat is a predator in the desert community of North Africa

A DESERT ANIMAL: THE CAMEL

No animal of the desert is better-known than the camel. Very few wild camels are left, but thousands of camels are raised by people in desert countries. Camels are used for transportation and hauling baggage.

A camel can go weeks without drinking water. A camel's hump, or humps, doesn't store water. The hump is made of fat. The camel's remarkable body can squeeze moisture out of almost anything it eats.

A camel can't store water in its hump, or humps, but it can still travel weeks without water

PEOPLE IN THE DESERT

Hundreds of thousands of people live in desert towns. By **irrigating,** or bringing in water, people have turned parts of deserts into **fertile** land.

Some tribal people, however, still live with their old ways. They live off the plants and animals of the desert, just as they always have.

In the Middle East, Bedouins herd goats, cattle, camels and sheep from place to place in the Sahara Desert. The Bedouins live in tents.

Bedouins ride their camels across the North African desert

HOW PEOPLE LIVE IN THE DESERT

People who live in deserts away from cities often live near an **oasis.** An oasis is a place with water.

At oasis villages, farmers raise crops such as barley, dates and wheat.

Desert people make clothing from the hides of their animals. Native Americans who live in the desert use desert plants for some of their food, medicine and home-building material.

Phoenix, Arizona, is a giant, man-made oasis in the Sonoran Desert

19

THE DESERT COMMUNITY

Each of the desert's plants and animals is part of a natural community. Each member of the community takes something from the community and gives something back to it.

Desert plants grow by changing sunlight into food and taking food from the soil. Some of the plant leaves, seeds, berries and stems become animal food. What isn't eaten **decays** and enriches the soil for new plants.

Some of the desert animals are **predators.** Predators, like coyotes and bobcats, hunt plant-eating animals.

Giant, treelike saguaro are the tallest cactus in the Sonoran Desert

A DESERT COMMUNITY: THE SONORAN

The Sonoran Desert is unusually rich in desert life. It is a habitat for insects, spiders, toads, snakes, lizards, birds and big desert animals — bobcats, mountain lions, coyotes, bighorn sheep and **peccaries.**

Each spring the Sonoran Desert's rocky ground blooms with a carpet of wildflowers. Red, pink and yellow cactus blossoms pop open. Spring days lure snakes and lizards from winter slumber. Birds search for nesting places in cactus and shrubs.

Deserts are dry, but not lifeless.

Glossary

decay (deh KAY) — to rot; the process by which dead plants and animals are broken down into tiny particles

fertile (FUR til) — referring to an area where plants grow easily

habitat (HAB uh tat) — the special kind of area where an animal lives, such as the *desert*

irrigate (EAR uh gate) — to supply more water to an area to grow better crops

nocturnal (nok TUR nal) — active at night

oasis (o A suss) — a fertile area in an otherwise dry region

peccary (PEHK uh ree) — a small, wild pig of the southwestern United States and parts of Mexico and Latin America

predator (PRED uh tor) — an animal that kills other animals for food

INDEX